SPORTS SUPERSTARS
ANTHONY EDWARDS

BY THOMAS K. ADAMSON

TORQUE

BELLWETHER MEDIA • MINNEAPOLIS, MN

Torque brims with excitement perfect for thrill-seekers of all kinds. Discover daring survival skills, explore uncharted worlds, and marvel at mighty engines and extreme sports. In *Torque* books, anything can happen. Are you ready?

This edition first published in 2026 by Bellwether Media, Inc.

No part of this publication may be reproduced in whole or in part without written permission of the publisher. For information regarding permission, write to Bellwether Media, Inc., Attention: Permissions Department, 3500 American Blvd W, Suite 150, Bloomington, MN 55431.

Library of Congress Cataloging-in-Publication Data

LC record for Anthony Edwards available at: https://lccn.loc.gov/2025013835

Text copyright © 2026 by Bellwether Media, Inc. TORQUE and associated logos are trademarks and/or registered trademarks of Bellwether Media, Inc. Bellwether Media is a division of FlutterBee Education Group.

Editor: Kieran Downs   Designer: Gabriel Hilger

Printed in the United States of America, North Mankato, MN.

TABLE OF CONTENTS

PLAYOFF WIN................................ 4
WHO IS ANTHONY EDWARDS? 6
OVERCOMING HARDSHIP 8
BECOMING AN NBA STAR 14
EDWARDS'S FUTURE 20
GLOSSARY 22
TO LEARN MORE 23
INDEX 24

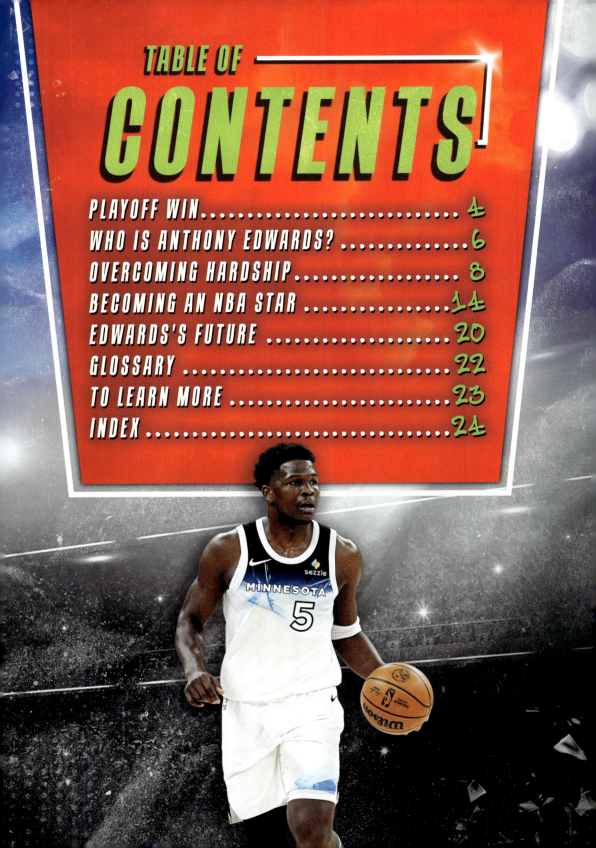

PLAYOFF WIN

It is Game 7 of the **semifinals** of the Western **Conference**. The Timberwolves have taken the lead after being down by 20 points.

The Timberwolves steal the ball. Anthony Edwards runs to the corner. His teammate passes him the ball. He shoots a wide open **3-pointer**. He scores! The Timberwolves take a 10-point lead! They move on to the Western Conference Finals.

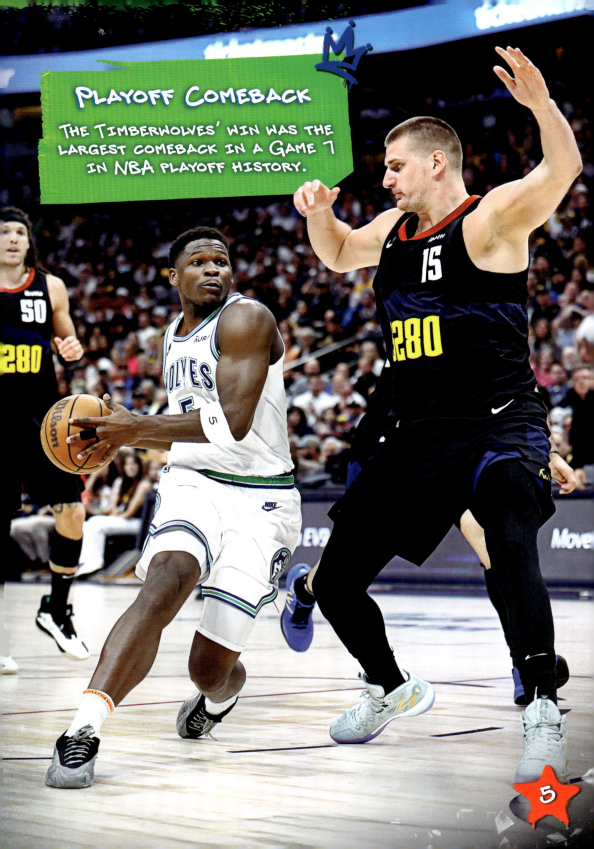

Playoff Comeback

The Timberwolves' win was the largest comeback in a Game 7 in NBA playoff history.

WHO IS ANTHONY EDWARDS?

Anthony Edwards is a **shooting guard** in the **National Basketball Association** (NBA). He quickly became the Minnesota Timberwolves' top player at a young age. He led the team to their first Western Conference Finals in 20 years.

ANTHONY EDWARDS

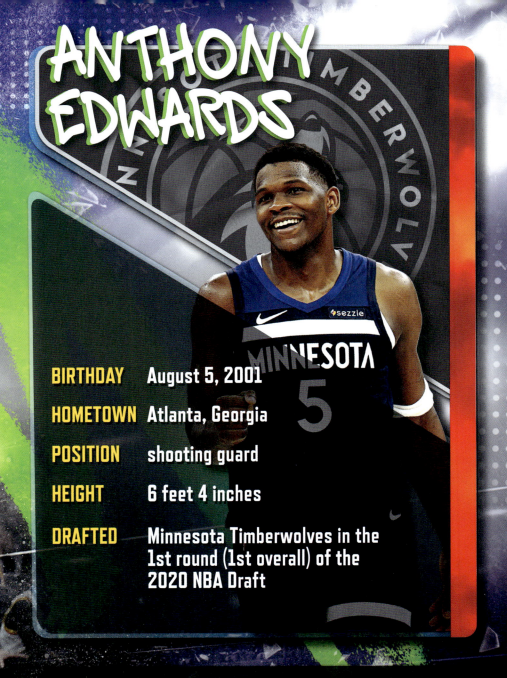

BIRTHDAY	August 5, 2001
HOMETOWN	Atlanta, Georgia
POSITION	shooting guard
HEIGHT	6 feet 4 inches
DRAFTED	Minnesota Timberwolves in the 1st round (1st overall) of the 2020 NBA Draft

His ball handling and shooting skills helped make the Timberwolves a winning team again. His exciting and powerful dunks have made him a superstar!

OVERCOMING HARDSHIP

Growing up, Edwards lived with his mom and siblings at their grandmother's house. Edwards played both football and basketball. He was a good **running back**. His mom was his biggest fan.

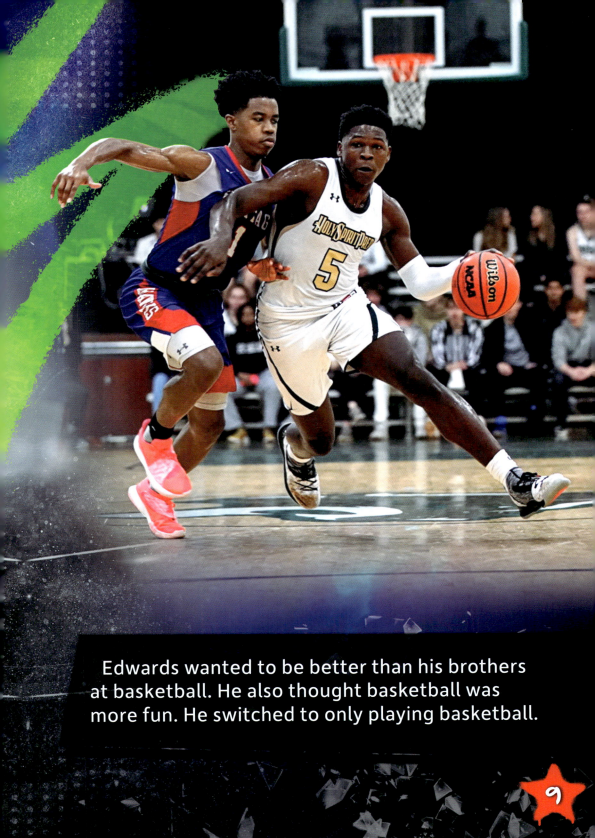

Edwards wanted to be better than his brothers at basketball. He also thought basketball was more fun. He switched to only playing basketball.

9

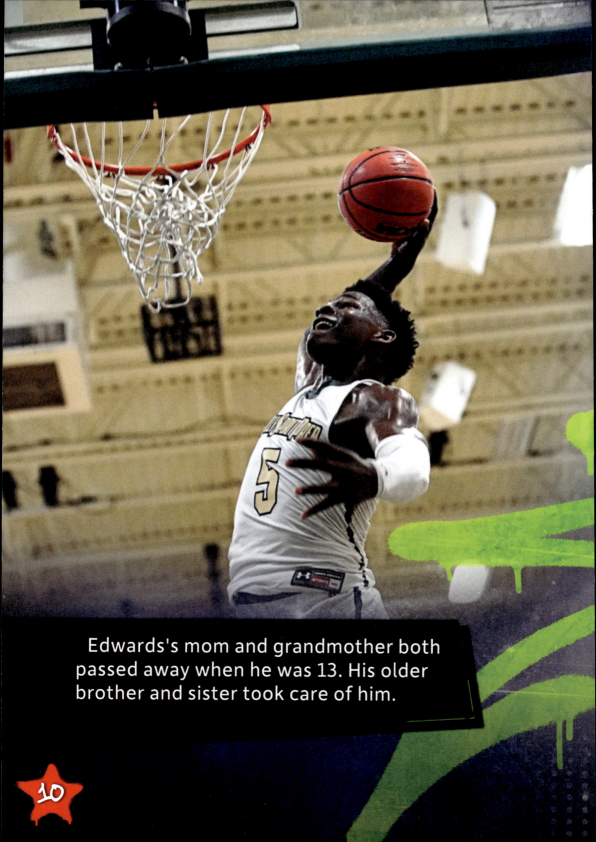

Edwards's mom and grandmother both passed away when he was 13. His older brother and sister took care of him.

10

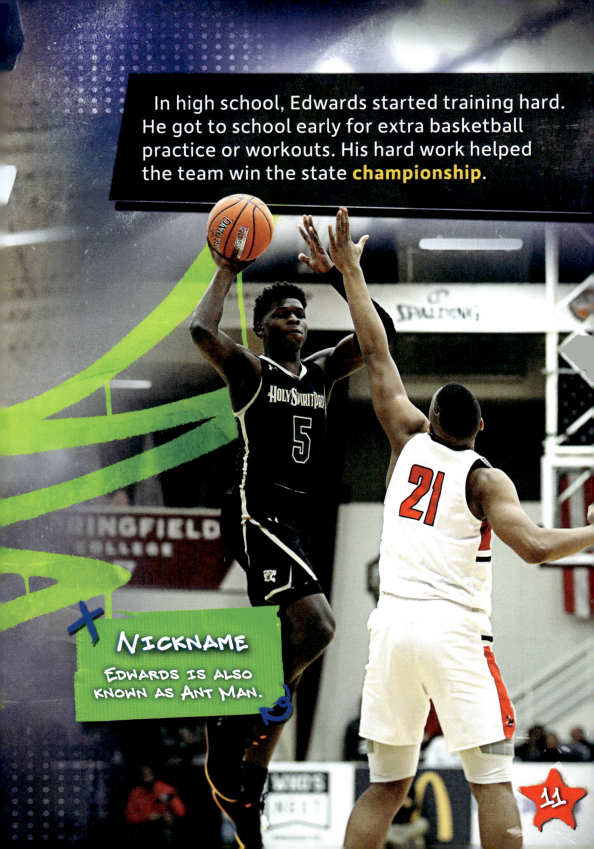

In high school, Edwards started training hard. He got to school early for extra basketball practice or workouts. His hard work helped the team win the state **championship**.

Nickname

Edwards is also known as Ant Man.

11

Edwards went to college at the University of Georgia. He played well in his **freshman** year. He was the leading scorer for the team. He scored 19.1 points per game and was named Freshman of the Year for his conference.

Edwards only played one year of college basketball. In 2020, he decided to enter the NBA **Draft**.

FAVORITES

MUSIC	SNACK	NBA PLAYER	PET

hip-hop	Chester's Hot Fries	Kevin Durant	English bulldog

BECOMING AN NBA STAR

2020 NBA DRAFT

The Timberwolves picked Edwards first overall in the 2020 NBA Draft. He scored 19.3 points per game in his **rookie** season. He was named to the NBA All-Rookie Team.

In his second year, he helped the Timberwolves make the **playoffs**. Edwards scored 36 points and had 6 **assists** in his first playoff game. But the Timberwolves lost the series.

ANTHONY EDWARDS MAP

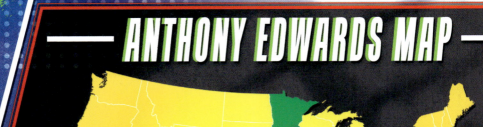

○ **Minnesota Timberwolves, Minneapolis, Minnesota**

2020 to present

2022 NBA PLAYOFFS

YOUNG ROOKIE
Edwards was only 19 years old when he played in his first NBA game.

15

In the 2022–2023 season, Edwards was named to his first **All-Star Game**. He led the Timberwolves to the playoffs again.

In Game 2 of the first round, Edwards scored 41 points. This set a team record for most points scored in a playoff game. But they lost the series.

2023 ALL-STAR GAME

In the 2023–2024 season, Edwards became a top NBA star. He averaged 25.9 points per game. He played in the All-Star Game again. He played well in the playoffs and led his team to the Western Conference Finals.

Edwards played for Team USA in the 2024 Paris **Summer Olympics**. He helped the team win a gold medal!

2024 WESTERN CONFERENCE FINALS

TIMELINE

— 2019 —
Edwards starts playing basketball at the University of Georgia

— 2020 —
Edwards is drafted first overall by the Timberwolves

— 2021 —
Edwards is named to the All-Rookie Team

2024 PARIS SUMMER OLYMPICS

Number 5
In 2023, Edwards changed his number from 1 to 5. This honors his mother and grandmother who both passed away on the 5th of a month.

— 2023 —
Edwards plays in his first All-Star Game

— 2024 —
Edwards helps Team USA win a gold medal at the Summer Olympics

EDWARDS'S FUTURE

Edwards helped start Don't Follow the Wave. This program helps students who play sports get started in sports businesses. Edwards also runs a free basketball camp for kids in Atlanta. He works on basketball skills with kids.

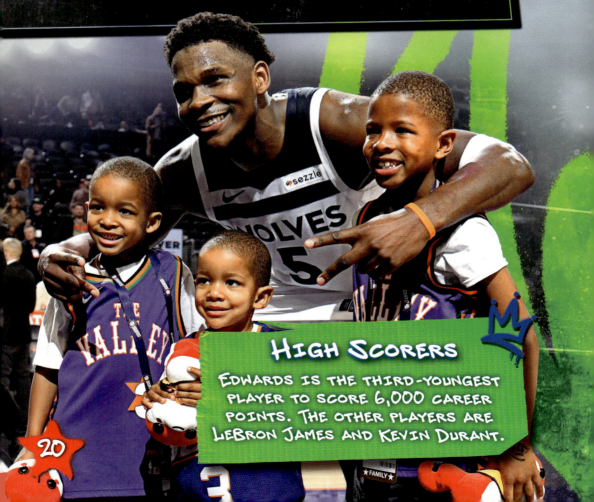

High Scorers

Edwards is the third-youngest player to score 6,000 career points. The other players are LeBron James and Kevin Durant.

Edwards is a popular player across the NBA. He wants to keep helping the Timberwolves win games!

GLOSSARY

3-pointer—a shot taken from behind a line that counts for three points instead of two

All-Star Game—a game between the best players in a league

assists—passes to a teammate that result in a score

championship—a contest to decide the best team or person

conference—a grouping of teams that often compete against each other

draft—a process during which professional teams choose high school and college players to play for them

freshman—a student in their first year of college

National Basketball Association—a professional basketball league in the United States; the National Basketball Association is often called the NBA.

playoffs—games played after the regular season is over; playoff games determine which teams play in the championship game.

rookie—a first-year player in a sports league

running back—a player on a football team who carries the ball on running plays

semifinals—the series of games played to determine which teams play in the final series of a sports tournament

shooting guard—a position in basketball where the player scores points by taking shots from far away from the basket

Summer Olympics—a worldwide summer sports contest held in a different country every four years

TO LEARN MORE

AT THE LIBRARY

Doeden, Matt. *Anthony Edwards vs. Dwyane Wade: Who Would Win?* Minneapolis, Minn.: Lerner Publications, 2026.

Doeden, Matt. *Meet Anthony Edwards: Minnesota Timberwolves Superstar.* Minneapolis, Minn.: Lerner Publications, 2026.

Whiting, Jim. *The Story of the Minnesota Timberwolves.* Mankato, Minn.: Creative Education, 2023.

ON THE WEB

Factsurfer.com gives you a safe, fun way to find more information.

1. Go to www.factsurfer.com

2. Enter "Anthony Edwards" into the search box and click 🔍.

3. Select your book cover to see a list of related content.

INDEX

All-Star Game, 16, 18
Atlanta, Georgia, 20
awards, 12, 14, 18
childhood, 8, 9, 10, 11
Don't Follow the Wave, 20
draft, 12, 14
family, 8, 9, 10, 19
favorites, 13
finals, 4, 6, 18
map, 15
Minnesota Timberwolves, 4, 5, 6, 7, 14, 16, 21
National Basketball Association, 5, 6, 12, 14, 15, 17, 18, 21
nickname, 11
number, 19
playoffs, 4, 5, 6, 14, 15, 16, 17, 18
points, 4, 12, 14, 16, 18, 20
profile, 7
semifinals, 4
shooting guard, 6
Summer Olympics, 18, 19
Team USA, 18
timeline, 18–19
trophy shelf, 17
University of Georgia, 12
Western Conference Finals, 4, 6, 18

The images in this book are reproduced through the courtesy of: Matt Krohn/ AP Images, front cover; Abbie Parr/ AP Images, p. 3; David Zalubowski/ AP Images, p. 4; C. Morgan Engel/ Stringer/ Getty Images, p. 5; Tony Avelar/ AP Images, p. 6; David Berding/ Contributor/ Getty Images, p. 7 (Anthony Edwards); Tony Avelar/ AP Images, p. 8; Kevin Liles/ Contributor/ Getty Images, pp. 9, 10; Gregory Payan/ AP Images, p. 11; Tribune Content Agency LLC/ Alamy Stock Photo, p. 12; Kevin Mazur/ Contributor/ Getty Images, p. 13 (hip-hop); The Image Party, p. 13 (Chester's Hot Fries); ZUMA Press, Inc./ Alamy Stock Photo, p. 13 (Kevin Durant); adogslifephoto, p. 13 (English Bulldog); David E. Klutho/ Contributor/ Getty Images, p. 13 (Anthony Edwards); David Sherman/ Contributor/ Getty Images, p. 14; Sam Wagner, p. 15 (Timberwolves stadium); Joe Murphy/ Contributor/ Getty Images p. 15 (Anthony Edwards); Pool/ Pool/ Getty Images, p. 16; Garrett Ellwood/ Contributor/ Getty Images, p. 17; David Berding/ Stringer/ Getty Images, p. 18 (2024 Western Conference finals); University of Georgia/ Wikipedia, p. 18 (Georgia logo); Minnesota Timberwolves/ Wikipedia, p. 18 (Timberwolves logo); Abaca Press/ Sipa USA via AP Images/ AP Images, p. 19 (2024 Paris summer Olympics); Sipa USA/ Alamy Stock Photo, p. 19 (2024); Barry Gossage/ Contributor/ Getty Images, p. 20; Christian Petersen/ Staff/ Getty Images, p. 21; Xinhua/ Alamy Stock Photo, p. 23.